Moritake Takeichi

The Wilderness

POEMS OF A YOUNG AINU

Translated by Gary Wyckoff

ROSE BOOKS

原始林

Foreword

Moritake Takeichi, whose Ainu name was 'Itakunoto', is known as one of the 'Three Great Ainu poets', along with Iboshi Hokuto and Batchelor Yaeko. He was born in the fishing village of Shiraoi in southwestern Hokkaido in 1902, the eldest son of Ehechikari (father) and Otehe (mother). His father passed away when he was still an infant and the family was thrown into poverty, a condition made worse by the fact that both his mother and grandmother were visually impaired. He started working in the local fishery at the age of 9 to help support his family. After graduating from elementary school in 1915 he left Shiraoi to work as a migrant laborer in the herring fisheries at Ishikari, Atsuta, Usuya (Obiracho) and Rumoi. When he reached the age of fifteen he returned to his native village where he was hired as a mail carrier, and two years later, in 1919, he became a porter at Shiraoi Station. In 1923, after four years of intensive self study, he took and passed the employment examination for the Sapporo Railroad and rose from temporary laborer to become an official permanent employee of the National Railway. This was a remarkable achievement for someone with only a primary school education, especially as the economy in those days was severely depressed and there were dozens of applicants for every available job. At the time Moritake joined the railroad it employed about 22,000 people in Hokkaido, of whom 10% were imperial appointments or graduates of Tokyo University. Thirty percent were permanent employees like Moritake, and the remaining 60% were temporary laborers. His rise within the Japanese system coincided with an increasing interest in assisting his fellow Ainu to escape from the suffering and poverty that afflicted them. Moritake served as freight manager at Oiwake, Tomikawa, Tomakomae and Shizunai stations. During this time he was elected union representative, a testament to the respect he had earned among his Japanese peers. A few years later he successfully completed the prestigious conductor training program; however, for reasons that are unclear, he was passed over and never did receive the promotion he was due. This appears to have marked a turning point in Moritake's life. In 1935 he abruptly resigned from his secure lifetime position at the railroad. Some have suggested that he was upset by the decision of the railroad to promote "Ainu tourism," or he may simply have become disillusioned by institutional discrimination. Be that as it may, he decided to sacrifice his own security and comfort to devote himself to the upliftment and revitalization of the Ainu community. He alludes to this transition in one of the tanka poems in this collection.

> Half my life I spent in selfish pursuits
> with the rest I shall serve the *utari*

After leaving the railroad Moritake returned to his native village of Shiraoi and tried to make a living as a fisherman. Later he and his wife opened a small restaurant. He passed away in 1976 at the age of 74.

Moritake was born in the 35th year of the Meiji Era (1902). The Meiji Restoration in 1867 marked Japan's entry into the modern age after a long period of feudalism and self-imposed isolation. The Meiji government embarked on a bold and ambitious program of expansion, development and modernization aimed at enabling Japan to both catch up with and fend off the western industrialized powers (including Russia). It was during this period that Japan annexed the Ryukyu Kingdom in the south, deposed its King, and established the Prefecture of Okinawa. Meanwhile, to the north, the land of Ezo was officially annexed by Japan in 1879 and its name was changed to Hokkaido. The Meiji government quickly embarked on a large-scale program of commercial, agricultural, and industrial development, and at the same time put in place a number of policies designed to Japanize the indigenous Ainu and train them to become loyal subjects of the imperial state. Like the Okinawans in the south, the Ainu were forced to give up many distinctive aspects of their culture, including their language, tattoos and religious ceremonies, but for the Ainu it did not stop there; they lost their very way of life. Their rights to hunt deer and fish for salmon were severely curtailed, and they were given small plots of land and encouraged to become farmers. Meanwhile displaced ex-samurai (*tondenhei*) were recruited to colonize and defend the newly annexed territory and these soldier-settlers descended on Hokkaido in waves during the late 1800s, displacing Ainu villages and eventually establishing some 40 settlements on the island. Forests were cut down in the name of agricultural development, a modern cannery facility was built and deer were hunted on an industrial scale, with the meat being sold to wealthy consumers in Tokyo. Overhunting and a series of severe winters drove the famed Ezo Sika (deer) to the brink of extinction, although today they have made a robust recovery. The Ezo wolf was not so fortunate. An imperial horse ranch was established in Nikkappu in 1888, and the native Ezo wolves, deprived of the deer which had been their natural prey, began to target the horses and sheep that had been imported to stock the royal farm. This could not be tolerated and a bounty system was implemented which resulted in the systematic poisoning of nearly 2000 wolves. The Hokkaido wolf had been completely wiped out by 1896.

This aggressive program of modernization did not only affect the deer and the wolves. As an example, at the beginning of Meiji there were around 200 Ainu families and 10 Japanese households in the vicinity of what is now Kushiro. A report from Kushiro to the government headquarters at Nemuro during the severe winter of 1879 reads, "To assuage their hunger the Ainu have been forced to go into the hills and dig out of the snow the remains of dead deer. They grind up the bones and boil them with a few peeled acorns. They have one bowl of this gruel in the morning and one in the evening. Many don't even have this much, and often go for days with no food at all." The government uprooted all the Ainu families in Kushiro and forcibly shifted them 30km to the north, to the area now known as Tsurui, to make way for a group of Japanese soldier-settlers from Tottori Prefecture. This pattern of forced eviction was repeated throughout Hokkaido.

As part of its development strategy, the Meiji government implemented a strict policy of ethnic assimilation in its two new prefectures, Okinawa and Hokkaido. In both places great efforts were made to Japanize the indigenous populations by suppressing their language, religion and cultural practices. Such a policy must have seemed perfectly rational to a Meiji government tasked with molding a unified modern state from a diverse and geographically disparate collection of relatively independent fiefdoms, but this policy of assimilation became the cause of great suffering to the Ainu people. On the one hand, the Ainu were given Japanese citizenship (although 'former Ainu' was entered into their family registers), so that they became Japanized from a legal standpoint. On the other, their language, culture and way of life were brutally suppressed. In 1899 an Aboriginal Protection Act was passed which gave up to five hectares of land to any Ainu willing to engage in agriculture, and the national government established schools and medical facilities in all Ainu villages of a certain size. Some twenty-five such "Aboriginal Schools" were established at this time, at which Ainu children were educated separately from their Japanese counterparts. Moritake was born in 1902, and an Ainu school called the "Hokkaido Prefectural Shiraoi Number 2 Normal School" was established in his native village in that same year. Use of the Ainu language was forbidden and all instruction was in Japanese. The curriculum focused on instilling 'loyalty and patriotism', and aimed to create faithful servants of Emperor and Empire. Prior to attending this school Moritake had grown up speaking only the Ainu language.

Ainu children and Japanese children would pass each other on the way to their respective schools, and the Japanese children would bully the Ainu children and call them names. Fights were common, and Moritake would often arrive at school bruised and bloodied. Finally his exasperated principal called him in and gave him a piece of advice. "It will do you no good to beat the Japanese with your fists. You need to study hard and defeat them with your mind." The Ainu and Japanese primary schools came together a few times each year for special events such as sports day or the school arts festival. It is said that one year Moritake memorized a story from one of his textbooks and recited it with great confidence and skill in front of the entire assembly. This had a great impact on the Japanese children, who came to realize that some of the Ainu pupils were actually quite clever. After this incident the Japanese schoolchildren reportedly stopped abusing Moritake and his companions.

In 1934 Moritake wrote and distributed a manifesto entitled "An appeal to the Ainu of Hokkaido" encouraging self-reliance and urging them to unite to promote mutual success and prosperity. The following year (1935), while still working for the railroad, he founded the Koseidoshikai, an association of young Ainu men aimed at revitalizing the downtrodden Ainu community. This organization was formed in Shizunai with the support and cooperation of Prefectural officials, the Mayor, the local school principal and the police chief, all of whom attended the opening ceremonies.

The Hokkaido Ainu Association was formed in 1946, soon after the end of the Second World War, and Moritake was named its executive director. This organization changed its name to the Hokkaido Utari Association in 1961, at which time Moritake was appointed a senior advisor, as well as Director of the newly established Showa-Shinzan Ainu Museum. In 1967 the Shiraoi Municipal Museum of History and Culture was established, and Moritake became its first Director. This museum may be considered the predecessor of the Upopoy National Ainu Museum and Park, which opened at lake Porotan near Shiraoi in July of 2020. (The Hokkaido Utari Association changed its name back to the Hokkaido Ainu Association in 2009).

Writer, Social Activist, and Poet

Mitsuoka Shin-ichi, the postmaster at Shiraoi, saw great promise in the young Moritake and hired him away from the herring fishery when he was 15. Mitsuoka was a scholar of Ainu history and culture, and both he and his wife Teruko were haiku poets. They took the young Moritake under their wing and introduced him to the world of haiku and tanka. A number of famous Japanese tanka poets are known to have visited Shiraoi village during this period, including Yosano Tekkan and his wife Kimiko, Saito Mokichi, and Maeda Yugure. It was in 1923, after he had begun working as a porter at the local railway station, that Moritake began to submit his own tanka to newspapers and literary magazines. He would have been 17 or 18 at that time. In 1927 he even started his own literary magazine 'Kinrei' (Silver Bell), which lasted for four issues, and two years later in 1929 he published another journal called 'Reimei' (Dawn). It was in that same year that Moritake, under the influence of Mitsuoka Teruko, joined the literary circle 'Aozora' (Blue Sky) and began to study in earnest under the well-known tanka poet Namiki Bonpei, from whom he received the pen name 'Chikudo'.

In 1937, two years after resigning from the National Railway, Moritake published the volume presented here, 'The Wilderness, Poems of a Young Ainu'. This was the first of only two books of poetry written by Moritake during his lifetime, the other being 'Ainu Tales Old and New', which came out in 1955. Most of his work was published in literary magazines and newspapers.

The Wilderness

Moritake's life spanned a period of rapid and intense change. A few decades before his birth Japan was still run by samurai warriors. Within the period of his lifetime Japan transformed itself from an isolated collection of feudal states into a modern industrial nation.

Great progress was achieved, but for the Ainu in particular this progress came at great cost. As one reads this collection of poems one is struck by the uninhibited and eclectic nature of his work. The first section of the book consists of verse poems in a variety of metrical styles. Some, influenced by classical Chinese patterns, are reminiscent of western romantic poetry in their use of figures such as nymphs and naiads to convey a wistful view of traditional Ainu life in ancient times, while others paint a brutally realistic picture of the desperate challenges that faced the new generation of Ainu in his day.

One sometimes runs across references to Moritake as one of the "three great poets of the Ainu resistance", but there is no indication that he considered himself to be a resistance poet. If one looks back on that period through the lens of our own post-war, post modern experience we are apt to miss the essence of his argument. A number of his poems were quite controversial.

Ainu Blood

> The tattoos round the mouths of the *menoko*
> and on the backs of their hands are slowly disappearing.
> The jet black Ainu beard
> has become a thing of the past.
> Ainu features are changing:
> intermarriage—
> mixed blood—
> assimilation—
> but if this is what is meant by extinction
> then I yearn for the extinction of our people,
> the sooner the better.
> Oppression, bullying

mockery and scorn —
I don't want to pass such a melancholy heritage
to my sweet children and grandchildren.
But remember—
even should Ainu features
disappear forever from this world,
Ainu blood!
will flow forever—
in the veins of the Japanese.

Here we see a man who deeply loves his people, and who feels an indescribable sense of loss as traditional Ainu culture gradually disappears, yet is not afraid to face the reality that a new age has dawned, and that the Ainu will have to buckle down and find a new way forward if they are to survive. His concerns are eminently practical. He rejects the prevailing tendency toward despair and defeatism. His is a positive message of self respect and self reliance. He does not tie his sense of humanity to superficial aspects of traditional Ainu culture, however much he may lament their passing. He rejects the notion of uniformity, and embraces the ideal of a just and pluralistic society. There is no need to suppress and destroy Ainu culture to make the Ainu into loyal citizens of Japan. The Ainu are already Japanese. Indeed, they are the original, the true Japanese, and they share with their ethnic Japanese neighbors a sincere and natural love for their homeland.

Yaeyama, 2020
Gary Wyckoff

The Wilderness

Preface

Although the Ainu people did not have a written language, from ancient times they had their own religious beliefs and had perfected their own arts. Their highest gods were those of fire, water, trees, and bears, but they revered and worshipped all things in the natural world. It was this type of religious sensibility that produced the legends associated with the Ainu Bear Festival, the idyll of the river nymph and the Ainu maidens, the tragic love story of the bear and the young Ainu woman and many others, some of which are reflected in the poems presented here. Stories and legends such as these were a fountainhead of inspiration that enriched the spiritual lives of the Ainu in peaceful times long ago.

Nowadays the Ainu people have the opportunity to receive a proper education, and their religious beliefs are gradually becoming modernized. Their sensibilities are being refined through exposure to newspapers, magazines and all the other instruments of modern civilization, and the old religious ceremonies and legends that have been passed on by word of mouth since time immemorial are being forgotten. Once the elders living today have passed from this world, many of the elements of our ancient heritage will be lost forever. As one who was born during this period of transition, on the one hand I am excited when I think of the opportunities for progress that assimilation into Japanese society will bring, but on the other I find myself overwhelmed by an indescribable sense of loss. It was nostalgia for this ancient heritage that inspired me to begin visiting the elders from time to time. I listened to them tell the old stories, and asked them about the ways of life, manners and customs of the Ainu in the old days. I made sure to participate in all of the old ceremonies so that I could experience them for myself, and in this collection of poems I have tried not only to describe these more traditional aspects of Ainu life, but I have also attempted to paint a frank and unvarnished picture of the feelings and experiences of the younger generation of Ainu, surrounded, as they are, by the excitement and distractions of modern society.

Despite my obvious lack of literary talent, the present work is, for me, a spiritual record, a cry from the heart that I could not suppress. I fervently long to see the day when the Ainu have completely merged into the modern, rational world, and the present work may be relegated to the status of a monument to a distant past.

Shiraoi, Hokkaido
Early summer, 1937
Moritake Takeichi

Table of Contents

Poems

Ainu Dance

Large bowls brimming with home-brewed saké
the *utari* drink, and then they dance, round and round
chanting mysterious songs, clapping softly
filling the long autumn night with *hoiyah, hoiya*

Ear hoops jangling, bright beads gleaming,
swords flashing, dancers leaping
till even the gods are pleased; dance on, round and round
filling the long autumn night with *hoiyah, hoiya*

The Nymph

I spied the lonely nymph who guards
this stream that wends through hill and dale,
past hamlet, farm and field, as she
looked up to the heavens and prayed:

"O starry Princess up so high
with magic sparkles in your eyes!
Smile down upon this lowly one,
and hearken to her tale.

How lovely were those times of old
when the pretty *pon-menoko* (young girls)
would carry down their *ninahi* (water buckets)
and morn and eve would call to me:

O shimmering river princess!
Tender-hearted river princess!
Please share with us a portion of
your beauty and your charm!

I loved those dear *pon-menoko*!
I always answered their sweet prayers,
and whispered softly in their ears
so they would know that I was there.

A thousand years have now gone by.
The *pon-menoko* come no more.
Though I still wait both morn and eve
what am I waiting for?

How empty is my broken heart!
I feel so utterly alone
by day I sigh, by night I wail,
bent low, like a drooping willow."

The star Princess poured out her love,
as she flashed swift across the sky,
and sought to sooth the naiad with
the twinkling of her eyes.

According to Nicolai Nevsky's "Ainu Folklore", human beings came into being as the result of intercourse between the Creator (God of the Land) and the Star Princess. Stars therefore represent the Mother Goddess in Ainu mythology.

Festival of the Bear

O sweet little bear cub!
your playground is now an immaculate white
purified by the snow,
and the many rich offerings
that you will carry
to our heavenly Father
are all waiting for you now before the *nusa* (altar)

your earthly mother
who nursed you at her own breast
and fed you with her own hand
she weeps to part with you
but her heart yearns to see you ascend
peacefully to heaven;

run, laugh and dance little cub
as flower arrows[1] rain down upon thee!
the *ekashi* (elders) are offering their *ongami* (prayers)
the *menoko* (women) are dancing
and the snow is falling, falling
as if to wipe your footprints from the earth

there is a great feast this night
all are reluctant to part
with you, *ka-mu-i-fu-tsu-chi* (the god of fire)
all the people in the *kotan* (village)
young and old, come together to celebrate
and fill the night with stories

[1] *These were ceremonial arrows specially carved and decorated as offerings for the bear to carry on to the next world. They did not harm the bear.*

the flames of the fire burn brightly
the sword flashes in the Ainu's hand
beads leap about the women's necks
ear hoops jangle through the night
till the dawn approaches
everyone is dancing, *hoiyah hoiya*

finally there are glimmerings in the eastern sky
kamui (the spirit of the bear cub)
is moved to the *shinda* (cradle)
above the *nusa* (altar)
the *otsukayo* (men) offer *ongami* (prayers)
and the *menoko* (women) *rimuse* (dance)

(one verse of the prayer says)

ra-tsu-chi-ta-ra	in peace
ka-mu-i, ko-tan	to the land of the gods
e-ko, ho-shi-bi-wa	make your return,
su-i	till
e-e-tsu, nan-go-ru-na	you come back to us again

as the solemn parting prayer
is offered to the Father of the Ainu
kamui ascends into the heavens
and lo! at the edge of the sky appears the morning star.
The people's hearts are filled with joy
as dawn breaks over the *kotan*.

Primitive life

Fire and water, plants and trees, birds and beasts
all were gods
to the *utari* (our ancestors) who lived long ago.
Theirs was a life of thankful prayer
Theirs was a life of faith!
I look back wistfully now
at the primitive life of my ancestors
who revered all things
and for whom all things were sacred.

Reminiscence

The fire dragon spews its flames
searing the heavens and scorching the earth
plants wither, dogs collapse
vapor rises from stones at the side of the road.

Hoping to cool off
I seek the edge of a wandering brook.
A refreshing breeze gently wafts
as I splash water on my hairy chest.

Sitting in the shade of the riverbank
cicadas in the treetops screeching noisily
sunlight sparkling on the flowing waters
my thoughts turned to times long past.

In the daytime the *utari* (our ancestors),
wearing *atsushi* (garment made of woven bark)
would have taken *marepu* (fishing spear) in hand,
and run to this spot to fish for salmon.

At night they built *sune* (fishing fires),
cast light upon the surface of the water
and caught the salmon that gathered there,
the *utari* (our ancestors), in days of old.

Refreshed, I awaken from my reverie,
just in time to see a small black bird
flit by along the surface of the stream—
an *utari* spirit, passing by?[1]

---

[1] The water ouzel is a small black river bird revered by the ancestors as a patron god of fishing and hunting.

Preparing the *Bushi*

Ainu takes down the soot-stained *ku* (bow)
and the *ikayopu* (quiver)
and prepares for the *ekimune* (hunt)
using secrets passed down from *michi* (fathers)
to mix the *suruku* (poison used in hunting)

Ainu takes a pinch
of *suruku* and places it on his tongue
waits in silence—
menoko motions to quiet the children
outside the snow piles up without a sound

silence—
every nerve focused
on his tongue
with keen sense
he analyzes the *suruku*

The ferocious bear,
that kills cow or horse with a single blow
the Ainu will bring him down
with the very tip of his tongue

Spring Lament

When the skylark sings and the warm winds blow
when young men's hearts begin to leap and bound
the girls of our village abandon us
to go to work in distant fishing grounds.

We watch helplessly as Spring's promises
lead all our innocent maidens astray
"All your hopes and dreams shall soon be fulfilled!"
Spring assures them as she lures them away.

The thrill of working with other young folk,
pulling the nets in the gathering swell
words of love whispered on warm balmy nights—
before long Spring has them under its spell.

O Spring! Why do you bring such joy and love
to all the birds, and the flowers and trees,
to the young couples in that far off land—
but such misery and sorrow to me?

O Spring! I loathe your melancholy days
I curse the dismal darkness of your nights.
To others you bring song and sweet romance
but you leave us here with no hope in sight.

The maid returns; she is heavy with child.
She walks out with her lover, hand in hand.
Look at her eyes! Don't they sparkle with joy?
Look how proud she is to show off her man!

O you *kotan* girls and your foolish loves.
Soon all your sweethearts will cast you away
you'll clutch fatherless children to your breasts,
and choke back sobs of regret and dismay.

Lost butterflies now wakened from a dream
back home they flutter in an aimless trance,
like faded petals of a seaside rose
withering slowly on a thorny branch.

Ainu Blood

The tattoos round the mouths of the *menoko*
and on the backs of their hands are slowly disappearing.
The jet black Ainu beard
has become a thing of the past.
Ainu features are changing:
intermarriage—
mixed blood—
assimilation—
but if this is what is meant by extinction
then I yearn for the extinction of our people,
the sooner the better.

Oppression, bullying
mockery and scorn—
I don't want to pass such a melancholy heritage
to my sweet children and grandchildren.
But remember—
even should Ainu features
disappear forever from this world,
Ainu blood!
will flow forever—
in the veins of the Japanese.

Death of an *Ekashi*

With snow-white beard
bushy eyebrows that covered his eyelids
back arched like a bow
the *ekashi* (grandfather)
up and died

akoru (our)
ekashi (grandfather)
pirika (good)
onne (died peacefully)
so the faces of the *utari* (our people)
are not sad

menoko (the women)
pound the *shito* (mochi)
ekashi (the old men)
make offerings of saké and speak of the old days
and the deeds of the departed one.
Beside the pillow of the *ekashi*
is a large *tsuki* (wooden bowl)
filled with saké.
A *kiseru* (pipe) leans against his cheek
from which *tanbaku* (tobacco) smoke
gently rises

a white birch *ku* (bow) and
ikayopu (quiver) hang from
the spear-shaped *kuwa* (burial marker)
that stands behind him.

These will continue
in the next life:
the Ainu and the *ekimune* (the hunt)

the ekashi's *tanbaku* has burned out
among the crowd is heard
the sobbing of the *menoko*
another Ainu is gone.
The *ekashi's* grandchild
born tomorrow
will carry some of his blood,
but he will be a *shisamu* (Japanese)
he will be a *shisamu*...

Burial Tablet

Lying beside the tiny corpse
the young *menoko* dries her weeping milk
with a bit of cotton cloth
hugs the cold child tightly to her breast
mad with grief she presses her cheek to his.
In the dim light of an electric bulb
the hood of the snow-white shroud peeks out
from the *menoko's* bosom

Around the burial tablet of white birch
various offerings are arranged
lamplight flickers gently
over the ashes of the dead fire
a dog howls lonely in the distance.
As midnight approaches
all are moved to tears
by the bitter sobs
of the *menoko* mother

Melancholy Stroll

Drawn by the fragrance of the acacias
I stroll with a friend
through town on a Sunday afternoon

fancy shop windows
voices on the radio
rumble of the streetcars
hoarse cries of perfume vendors
the sweaty crowd

salaried men, students
strutting "modern girls"
bright summer streets

then weaving through the throng
all dressed in white, comes a foreign-looking face.
My companion jerked his chin in disdain
"Look" he said, "there goes a Korean"
following the white figure
with an icy stare

———

These simple words, so nonchalant
turned all my joy to sadness,
and cast a deathly shadow on my soul

Lily Bells

For your graceful lines
and delightful fragrance
all the young men
admire you
hold you to their cheeks
press you to their lips
how very blessed you are
you lily bells!

But when the dawn comes
your perfume vanishes
your form withers
your colors fade
and those who yesterday
loved you so
now without a thought
toss you out by the wayside.

O ill-fated beauties! The fairest flowers
are the first to fade. Life is too short
to spend grieving
over this cold and cruel world.
Pleasure is short lived,
but sorrow endures.

Destiny

One man!
Awakening from a long night's dream
looks into the distance
and on the far horizon
sails raised, riding the following winds of progress
slicing through the waves of civilization
he sees the shadows of a host of ships.
Ah! We have been sleeping far too long.
"Oh *utari* brothers, hurry, rise up
we too must seek the shores of this new civilization."

Shining in the light of the setting sun
the weary faces of the *utari*
burn with hope
hearts athrill with dreams of a glorious future
defying the blasts of evil customs
plowing through waves of convention
with manly courage upon society's stormy seas
together we embark, but all too soon …

"The path ahead is looking dark,
ominous clouds are gathering."

The hardships of life assault us like a tempest;
tossed about by an onrushing flood of ridicule
soon the rudder of justice is broken
the sails of our resolve are torn
we are left floating wretched on the sea.

Hearts and souls exhausted, my brothers
cry out in desperation toward the distant shore,
the haven of their abandoned hopes

"The *utari* are half-dead,
the living are gasping for breath."

I embrace my broken-spirited brothers
and we abandon our fate to the God of Destiny.
Drifting, aimless, among the waves
we can only wonder where we will be cast ashore.
Will it be a land of desolation and despair?
A paradise of light and hope?— or
will we be sucked into a struggle for power
and dragged down to humanity's lowest depths?

Houses

Another house built with milled lumber is going up in the *kotan*.
Can any joy compare with this?
As for myself, I often think
that even if I were wealthy
I would still like to keep this hut of grass
just as it is
but when I think of how most people
hold us up to ridicule
because we live
in these primitive thatched huts
I say to the *utari* (the people),
let us encourage each other to save money
and build proper houses
to leave to our descendants.

Migrant Labor

There is a commotion
as of soldiers being sent off to war.
Children calling out for their fathers—
fathers looking for their children
this is the waiting room at the station on the day
the *utari* (the people) set out on their journey

"Take good care of yourself!"
"I'm counting on you to watch over things while I'm away!"

A shrill blast of the train's whistle signals the sad farewell—
handkerchiefs wave out of train windows
children yelling
the eyes of the *menoko* mist over.

After the men have left
the *kotan* (village)
feels desolate and dark

For the burial the *menoko*
has to carry the body and dig the grave herself,
oppressed with grief and loneliness.
The eyes of the children, the women, the elders
are filled with anxiety—
this year, again
the *utari* all sigh at the news of a poor catch
and wonder how they are going to survive.

Elegy

We lift the cold body of our friend
as the sun begins to set
and walk slowly toward the foot of the mountain.
Natural selection… survival of the fittest…

Alas, who can understand the grief
of the last members of a dying race?
hot tears flow unchecked
down our cheeks

the slopes above are thick with bush clover
depressions here and there mark graves fallen into decay
the wails of the grieving *utari*
cause the nearby burial markers to quiver

here is a marker shaped like a spear
fitting for an Ainu
whose hot blood knew the thrill
of hunting the great bear

here a marker in the shape of a needle
made for a *menoko* (woman)
who took great pride
in her skill at embroidery

here a sickle
marks the grave of a young infant.
It is meant to ward off evil spirits
and keep the soul from going astray

I think of my dear parents
and so many other *utari* buried here
now gone forever
and sink deeper into grief

the body of our departed friend
is gently lowered to its resting place
in a corner of the cold earth:
now the *utari* weep and wail

in the deepening twilight
the *ekashi* (old grandfather) cries out these words:

"Cross the great divide
we are strangers to you now
you have no mother or father
no brothers or sisters in this world.
Do not look back— go straight on
return to the land of your grandparents
make haste, god speed, farewell"

the body is slowly lowered into the earth
sobbing and lamenting
tears flow down the mourners cheeks
and drop like dew upon the corpse.
As his spirit leaves this nether world behind
the *utari* fall upon their knees,
and together we all weep

Above the tear-stained grave,
the *ekashi* erect the burial marker
as the sun sinks below the crest of the western hills.
O my friend! Farewell!

In the gathering darkness we carry our grieving hearts
back down the narrow path.
Wearily, in silence
we return to the kotan.

Yamase [3]

There is not a breath of wind,
but from the east a wall of dark gray clouds
is rushing toward us like a flood.
The evening sea is smooth as glass

The *utari* turn their gaze to the skies
tomorrow the *yamase* (east wind) will blow; they tie up their boats
plovers cry and wheel along the dusky strand
The evening sea is smooth as glass

The Echo

"By day the sound of the woodman's ax[1]
began to drive me mad, and by night I choked
on the ash and smoke of the bodies of their dead.[2]
Unable to bear it I have fled to these mountains."

The wood nymph gazed wistfully
toward the far off *kotan*
as she shared with me her memories
of happier days gone by.

"It was calm there even when blizzards blew.
In spring the *menoko* would come
to gather sticks of firewood in my garden
twittering like a flock of birds

Dreaming of love,
bright eyes ablaze, the *pon-menoko*
would cross their arms over their breasts
and fill the woods with tender melodies

Their throbbing hearts
burned with such love and passion
that they thrilled my soul—
like songbirds celebrating the arrival of spring

And when the young *menoko*
with quavering voices sang melancholy songs
in memory of departed fathers and mothers
or lost loves,

[1] In the old days the Ainu lived in the embrace of the primeval forest, where never the sound of an ax was heard.   [2] The Ainu traditionally had no custom of cremation.

I grieved with them, even as
I grieved with the trees in the forest
groaning in the whirling winds
of great storms.

Sometimes on spring days
as the young *menoko* chatted happily
I would sneak up quietly
to hear them gossip about the young Ainu men

But now the clamor of his ax
and his suffocating smoke
have driven me here, to this remote spot
in the heart of these mountains.

The *menoko* will not come this far
but sometimes on a breezy autumn day,
I can almost hear their harps playing in the trees
and I am reminded of those happy times."

Commemoration

1. How brave this crew from the land of the East,
   how weighty the mission they must fulfil
   to open a new air route to the south
   bridging Asia and the lands of Europe

2. O gallant youths, dashing, fearless and bold!
   Take this proud aircraft, all made in Japan,
   given the solemn name: "Kamikaze"[3]
   Go, and set a glorious world record

3. Let the lands of Europe marvel once more
   at the culture and spirit of Japan,
   the bastion and defender of the East.
   Go, extol the glories of our Empire

4. Though obstacles may try to block your way
   recall the roar of our passionate cheers,
   O sons of gods, from the land of the gods,
   arise with pride your duty to perform!

5. The skies are clear as we call our farewells
   raising our voices in thunderous song
   wings gleam in the light of the rising sun
   peace be with you on the journey ahead.

(Late February 1937; poem commemorating the record-breaking flight sponsored by the Tokyo Asahi Newspaper Co. linking Asia and Europe (Tokyo to London))

---

[3] *Divine wind*

Tanka

Welcome Party for Moritake Chikudo
(A gathering of the members of the Aozora Poet's Society
in Otaru at the home of Bonpei Namiki, October 26, 1934)

Chikudo my friend, you have journeyed far
what tales your cups will tell this cool fall night!

The *utari* must make it clear to all
they too are proud defenders of Japan

The shadowed cheek, the shoulders broad, behold!
Utari power shines for all to see!

Namiki Bonpei

They call us 'Ainu aborigines'
Chikudo, your brothers need you, arise!

How dazzling, how intense the flame of hope
that blazes up so brightly in his eyes!

Nomura Yasuyuki

From far Hidaka comes the scion's cry
"Our people are fading! Don't let them die!"

Throw off this sleep! He takes us by the arms
and roars with all the passion in his soul!

How bravely does this poet sound his call
how sad we all shall be to see him go

Mizugami Kouhei

The blood that boils in our *utari* veins
Chikudo turns into love for mankind

From Hidaka rings pure the poet's song,
Moritake's cry, "Save the *utari*" !

Seiko Okamoto

Meeting a new friend, passing round our cups
how the brisk night thrills to the poet's voice!

Aoyama Yukiji

What memories those broad shoulders evoke
in this mountain hut of an autumn eve

You are giving voice to a dying race
you took our hands in yours and gave us hope

Araya Tomio

In the sleet, puffing on a cigarette
Chikudo climbs the hill to Namiki's

Mizukubo Rin

With Chikudo now in this hilltop hut
it's as if Iboshi were here again

Inabata Shouji

We thrilled to see the shadow of our guest
darken the wall beside our Teacher's gate

Sotoyama Minoru

No condescension here, no cool disdain
you've filled my heart with hope this autumn eve

Moritake Chikudo

Cry from the Heart!

Why do we *utari* abase ourselves?
We must live as equals, with self-respect

Utari! Abandon this self-pity
by our own efforts we must find our way

If they lag behind in knowledge and skill
let the young *utari* struggle and strive!

The *utari* are living hand to mouth
We must combine our forces to survive

Be resourceful! Last spring I talked till dawn
with friends who plan to start a rabbit farm

Utari, how long will you sleep? Arise,
we must blaze a new trail to the future!

Utari, we have no more time to waste
we must wake up, stand up, or go extinct

How fervently I've raised this eager cry!
Now patient and alone I wait reply

If even one *utari* would rise up
in each village, ready to serve this Cause!

If only Hokuto were still alive!
Many are the nights I lament his loss.[4]

<hr>

[4] *Hokuto Iboshi (1901 –1929) was an Ainu waka poet and social activist. He devoted his life to improving the standing of the Ainu people.*

Half my life I spent in selfish pursuits
with the rest I shall serve the *utari*

At my hometown they've put up a new sign:
"Ainu village"— I cringe and turn away.

The times have changed; why do we still have these
degrading names, this discrimination?

They still refuse to close our 'native' schools,
convinced that Ainu children can't keep up

Visitors to these 'Ainu' schools seem shocked
to find that our children know how to read

The men have all left for the herring grounds
the *kotan* is desolate, cold and dark

and now the deadly cough has struck again
we're dropping like blighted leaves in spring winds.

Is this how the *utari* will die out?
In dark houses, lungs ridden with disease?[5]

Can I ever describe the woeful cries
of these wretched women grieving their dead?

I stand amidst the weeping and wailing,
wondering how we will ever survive

---

[5] *The Ainu experienced an acute epidemic of tuberculosis in the last decades of the nineteenth century and the first two of the twentieth. They had no natural resistance and their mortality rates from this disease were among the highest in the world. Some believed that the disease was caused by the lack of light in their houses.*

Can nothing be done? This horrid plague
is killing the *utari* one by one

Would that a Gandhi, a Christ, a hero
might arise among us in sacrifice

Girding his loins, he would thrust out his chest
take our hands in His and fill us with strength

He would unite our hearts, set them ablaze
lead us out from darkness into the light

But each time we think our hero has come
disease strikes him down and takes him away

No salmon in the rivers, no bear in
the hills, no land to till; where shall we go?

Slowly we *utari* begin to see—
our salvation lies in fields and paddies

Let us all reflect on our wretched lives
and resolve to build a better future

They scoff at our lack of education
now is the time to show that we are men

Pen dipped in boiling blood I raise this cry
to all *utari* youth, awake, arise!

Self-reproach

My professor heard I had stopped drinking
and wrote a message of encouragement

"That's the spirit, be firm in your resolve.
Dedicate yourself wholly to this Cause."
                                    (Dr. Kida)

I answered the call and arose to serve
but then the New Year's season rolled around

What's wrong with me? Why can I not refuse
when the *utari* passes me a cup?

I, who so often have implored others
to try and give up this evil habit

Never able to resist temptation
how disappointed I am in myself

When I call the *utari* to arise
is it really just the saké talking?

Visit to Chikabumi Village

The *utari* of Chikabumi called
for the return of their ancestral lands

and when spring arrived I rushed to join them
as they celebrated their great success

Long had I yearned to visit this *kotan*
how I enjoyed that first evening with friends

Kawamura the elder was my guide
we toured their lands, their path to the future

With such joy the *utari* welcomed me;
that night we drank and danced till nearly dawn…

But to see our Bear Festival performed
before a curious throng of tourists…

And to see them crowd our *utari* girls
asking eagerly for their autographs…

And *utari* men carving bears for sale…
mixed were my feelings on the long road home

On Days that I Shave

On days I don't shave I feel so exposed
I lose every time I try to play *go*[6]

Our elders took great pride in their long beards
now their descendants are troubled by them

Even when late and have to skip breakfast
bright are the mornings on days that I shave!

I feel so refreshed, my steps are so light
as dawn gently breaks, on days that I shave!

If people stare as I go on my way
I can stare right back, on days that I shave!

How cheerful I feel, I make people laugh
so fine is my mood, on days that I shave!

[6] Go is an abstract strategy board game for two players. The game was invented in
China more than 2500 years ago.

Night in the *Kotan* (village)

In a thatched hut, in spine-shivering cold
an old man recounts tales of ancient times

His cloudy eyes sparkle in the firelight,
spirits warmed by a cup of hot saké

Below an oil lamp, his white beard aglow
he tells of battles with bears long ago

Beard swinging wild from side to side, he slaps
the hearth; we listen spellbound as he speaks

of times when men kept company with gods.
He brings our myths and legends back to life.

Today again the *Yamase* blew strong
the *utari* groan, their cupboards are bare

Will the winds shift tomorrow? At the beach
I see two or three men eyeing the sky

This year's herring catch was so poor our men
need train fare home; whatever shall we do?

No songs fill the lonely *kotan* tonight
all is still save the distant howls of dogs

Songs for Shibechari

A shrill whistle sounds; it seems a freighter
is approaching the Shibechari beach

From villages near and far the young men
come to unload the freight, the beach is thronged

The steamer departs, and the *utari*
stumble home, drunk. I heave a sorry sigh.

Most of what they earned they've spent on saké
what will they do for money tomorrow?

For these men drink is their only pleasure
sometimes I feel I can hardly blame them

There's been an accident at the racetrack
Aoyama the jockey has been hurt[7]

Alas, our prayers to the gods were in vain
that night the sad news comes that he has passed

All of us left here in paradise lost
pray that he will protect us from above

At dusk the river's riffles tell their tales
of ancestors who lived here long ago

[7] *Aoyama Ichinoshin was a famous Ainu jockey. His death at the Nakayama racetrack was a bitter blow to his fellow utari.*

Along the banks of the Shibechari
thin plumes of smoke from *kotan* rooftops rise

Tourists who visit the *kotan* say these
modern roofs destroy the "local color"

Swords flash as the rain pours, *ho-i ho-i*
the *utari* mourn the death of a friend

As the crickets chirp I can't help wonder
what will be the future of my people?

An *utari* lies drunken by the road
there an *utari* preacher stops to pray

(*Rev. Kondo*)

Don't give up! We must struggle to be saved!
We listen spellbound through the long dark night

White *furoshiki* wrapped around their heads
young *utari* women plough the dark earth

Beside the ploughing women puppies play
and frolic as the soaring skylarks sing

How masterfully they handle the reins
amazed I stop to marvel at their work

Bright red roses in *utari* gardens
waft soothing scents along the twilight streets

In the next city council election
let's put up an *utari* candidate

People say the *utari* will vote for
anyone who will give them a free drink

Don't fall into temptation, don't be fooled
by drink; *utari*! use your vote wisely

All through Hokkaido *utari* names rang;
the town council election is over

This time finally we have won a seat;
We've pulled ourselves up by our own bootstraps!

(Election of Mr. Sotoyama)

Beneath his ruined castle Saksaynu
himself is smiling on this happy day![8]

[8] *Saksaynu was a 17th century Ainu chief who fought against the Matsumae clan during the Edo period. His defeat marked the end of military Ainu resistance to Japanese incursion.*

Tanka from the School Excursion
(August 1936, Shiraoi Primary School field trip to Sapporo)

The children are in a frolicsome mood,
running ahead, cheering the rice farmers

Gear, bedding in perfect order; world class
Japanese military discipline
(Upon visiting the military barracks)

Dreadful, blood stained, bullet-torn war relics
first-hand proof of the Yamato spirit!
(Yamato damashi, visit to the historical museum)

Children, foreheads to the ground, pray before
the Souchinshu shrine for a safe journey

The children stand before the camera
this happy day shall never be forgot

Printing press, showing the world as it is,
and delivered to our homes tomorrow
(Visit to the Times newspaper)

Hope sparkles brightly in the children's eyes
as they enter among the dark green elms
(Visiting the campus of Hokkaido University)

Red roof tiles mark the Hokkai garrison
the children circle round to show respect

Learning about radio broadcasting,
so many sound effects! JOIK

Racing through supper, rushing the teachers
Tonight they will visit the cinema!

Recent Poem

The newspapers are all making a fuss
one lone *utari* has earned a degree

Now if they would only stop using the
word Ainu we would be getting someplace

If you want to find true Ainu spirit
look to our heroes and our history

The revised Protection Act has been passed
I ask the young *utari* what they think

The revision has only made things worse
in two or three years our lands will be gone

When we are reduced to begging will they
say we have now achieved equality?

To those who think we still need protection
to keep our lands, I say 'Don't be a fool!'[9]

It would have been enough to abolish
"Ainu" schools, such is my impassioned cry

Protection equals discrimination
O young *utari*! Stand up for yourselves!

---

[9] *The so-called "Protection Act" placed limitations on what the Ainu could do with their property, and in fact opened the way for the Ainu to be dispossessed of what little land they had been given.*

詩編「アイ×エは踊る」參照

Ainu Dance

Festival of the Bear

Death of an Ekashi

詩篇「輓歌」參照

Elegy

Translator's Note

I had the privilege of meeting Moritake Takeichi's adopted son Umegae Kazutomo in 1983, only a few years after my wife and I had settled in Japan. We were idealistic young Baha'is, eager to change the world, and Umegae-san was already an old man with a gray beard and a heart ablaze with love for his people and for mankind as a whole. In the early 60s both he and his father had embraced the Baha'i cause, which recognizes the oneness of mankind and calls for the creation of a new world civilization characterized not by uniformity, but by the principles of justice and mutual respect. When we first met Umegae-san he was traveling around Japan giving lectures on Ainu history and culture. He came to our home when he visited Kyushu and we had the honor of having him stay with us on several occasions. For some reason he took us under his wing and we became part of his family. Physically he was not healthy, but spiritually he was a fountain of inspiration. He suffered from diabetes and had a dialysis port in his arm. For the last few years of his life he would spend six weeks in a hospital in Hokkaido gathering his strength, then he would travel around the country until he collapsed, at which point he would return to Hokkaido and repeat the process. He gave thousands of Japanese the opportunity to connect with a 'real' Ainu and discover that Ainu culture was still alive and well despite government denials and the lack of official recognition. The last time Umegae-san visited our home he took a book out of his bag and handed it to me as he was leaving. It was 'Lelakorachi', a collection of his father's works that had been compiled posthumously and published in 1976. "You like poetry," he said. He pointed out the facsimile copy of *Genshirin* (The Wilderness) and said, "Someday I'd like you to translate these into English." At the time I was conversant in Japanese but was far from literate. I could not read the book, let alone translate it. The book was packed away and forgotten.

Nearly twenty years later we relocated to Yaeyama, and the long lost book resurfaced. Once we had settled in our new location I made a rough translation but found myself unable to access the source and reference materials I needed to complete the work, so once again I set the manuscript aside. Fast forward another nineteen years. The creeping tentacles of the internet had finally reached even to our isolated village, and made it possible for me to do the research necessary to complete the translation. Despite its obvious inadequacies, it is my hope that this small volume may serve to introduce to the English-speaking world a great poet and truly remarkable man, a man who was not only instrumental in helping to uplift the Ainu people and preserve their culture, but who also helped set in motion the process that led the Japanese government in 2019 to officially recognize the Ainu as an indigenous people of Japan. Some may say 'too little too late', but for a country like Japan, which has for so long based its very identity on the myth of racial homogeneity, to finally start to come to grips with this issue is a truly remarkable and praiseworthy development. One senses that this could not have happened had it not been for the patience, dedication, courage, sacrifice, perseverance, passion and eloquence of Moritake Takeichi. Future generations will marvel at the historical and literary legacy that he has left behind.

Yaeyama
Early summer 2020
Gary Wyckoff

ROSE BOOKS

**The Wilderness
Poems of a Young Ainu
by Moritake Takeichi**

First edition – October 19, 2020
Translation: Gary Wyckoff
Graphic Design: André Geßner

Translated from the original 1937 edition issued privately by Moritake Takeichi under the imprint of the Shiraoi-Pirika Poetry Society and is published here with the permission of Moritake Emiko. Facsimile is from the original edition, as reproduced in Lelakorachi (Like the Wind), Moritake's collected works, except that the page numbers match those in the compilation. Cover art adapted from the original 1937 edition. Artist unknown.
Historical photos are from the original 1937 edition. Photographer unknown. Photograph of Moritake Takeichi (p. 17) by Kakegawa Genichiro (courtesy of Takenaga Makoto, Director of the Sendaihan Shiraoi Motojinya Museum). For biographical material I am indebted to Yamamoto Yujou of the Moritake Takeichi Research Society.

Footnotes in italics were added by the translator. All others are by the author.

Published by Rose Books
www.rosebooks.net
info@rosebooks.net
Tel. (+81) 0980-89-2765

ISBN 978-4-947713-00-1